SUPERCARRIER

Christopher Bennett

Motorbooks International
Publishers & Wholesalers

Library of Congress Cataloging-in-Publication Data
Bennett, Christopher
    Supercarrier / Christopher Bennett.
      p. cm. --(Motorbooks International
enthusiast color series)
    Includes Index.
    ISBN 0 7603--0166-2 (pbk. : alk. paper)
    1. George Washington (Aircraft carrier) II.
    Title. II. Series:
  Enthusiast color series.
  VA65.G46B46   1996
  356.9'435'0973--dc20   96-13068

On the front cover: The George Washington's nuclear reactors power its massive hull through the Atlantic with full authority.

On the frontispiece: A bird's-eye view of CVN-73, the men working the deck and performing a FOD walk-down, providing an indication of just how big this awesome nuclear-powered carrier really is. Clearly visible is the angled deck, which is bracketed by double white lines and with a yellow and white center line. This is so designed to permit aircraft to land, and if necessary overshoot, without colliding with others parked up on and around the bow and starboard waist areas. The two parallel bow catapult tracks are also visible, behind each of which are their JBDs. The waist cats are located to the right-hand side, running on a slightly converging angle. *US Navy*

On the title page: Each aircraft carrier is assigned a battle group, which exists essentially to support and protect the carrier. The number and type of vessels in such a battle group will vary but usually consists of some 12 to 14, including destroyers, Aegis guided-missile cruisers, attack submarines, supply ships, and perhaps even a smaller ASW helicopter carrier. *US Navy*

On the back cover: Even a huge aircraft carrier can pitch and roll in the ocean swells. The crew keeps the aircraft, like this F-14 Tomcat, chained to the deck when not in use.

Printed in Hong Kong

Contents

Introduction

"When word of a crisis breaks out in Washington, it's no accident that the first question that comes to everyone's lips is: 'Where is the nearest carrier?'"

— President Bill Clinton
Aboard USS Theodore Roosevelt

In the past there have been numerous photo-based books dedicated to US Navy aircraft carriers, of which the vast majority restrict their coverage largely to flight-deck action. Although the flight deck of a US Navy carrier is one of the most dynamic places to be, and ideal for action photography, this really is only half of the story.

With upward of 6,000 people on board, the modern nuclear aircraft carrier (CVN) is a kind of seaborne community, equipped with many of the domestic, life-sustaining facilities taken for granted on land. Within this book I've tried to take you behind the scenes on the USS *George Washington* (CVN-73), showing not just the flight-deck action, but a little of what life is really like aboard this amazing floating city.

Now that my short voyage aboard the *GW* is but a memory, I'd like to take this opportunity to thank the entire crew for their thoughtfulness and kindness toward this visiting stranger. At all times I was greeted with both courteousness

and a warm welcome, factors that go a very long way toward putting a CVN "first timer" at ease, in this (for me) strange, but awesome and wondrous world.

Throughout my photographic career I have worked with numerous varied military establishments around the globe, but in all honesty, I really cannot think of any that match the enthusiasm, dedication, and raw team spirit displayed so obviously aboard the USS *George Washington*. For the many, many of you who acknowledged my presence with a smile and a word, I thank you for making this an experience of a lifetime. I only hope that this book, the culmination of my endeavors, will suitably reward and compliment your obvious high level of excellence.

There's insufficient room available here to recognize everyone who contributed in the production of my book. However, I would like to thank the key players involved individually. These people include Lt.Cdr.

Mark McDonald, Chief Petty Officer Scott Mohr, and Tom Gelsanliter and his colleagues in the public-affairs office on the *GW*. I know how busy you guys were, and I really do appreciate the fact that you always made time to both advise me and guide me through the labyrinth world of CVN-73.

Also a very special thank you must go to the commanding officer of CVN-73, Captain Mal Branch for permitting me to set foot in this exclusive world; it's been a rare privilege. Thanks also to Captain Ron McElraft (CAG), Captain Pat Twomey (air boss), Commander Gerry Mauer (navigator), Commander Pete Williams (skipper of VF-143 "World Famous Dogs"), Lt. Chris "Basher" Blaschum (LSO VF-143), Lt. Jimmy McLaughlin (handler), Lt. Tom Chorlton (cat and arrestor gear officer), Lt. Marcus "Starch" Smallwood (VAW-121), Lt. Jeff "Toss" Lewis and Lt. Brian "Snapper" Hennessey (VFA-136), Lt. Steve "Shoe" Kelly (VA-34), and Chief Petty Officer Rick Davis. Also "cheers" to the *George Washington*'s photo shop for helping me out with Kodachrome film when my own reserve ran dry.

Last, but very important, my sincere thanks goes to Commander Kevin Wensing and Lt. Commander Fred Mertyl of the AIRLANT public-affairs office at Norfolk, Virginia. Commander Wensing expended considerable time and effort in ensuring both my visit and embark ran like clockwork. Without his help, this book simply would not have been possible.

To all those who call the USS *George Washington* home: Until we meet again, bon voyage CVN-73; may your cruise be both successful and fulfilling.

All images reproduced within this volume were shot exclusively with Nikon F4 cameras fitted with Nikkor lenses ranging from 16 to 300 millimeters, and on Kodak Kodachrome 64 film stock. Additional camera equipment was supplied by KJP Ltd. of London.

—*Christopher Bennett*

Chapter One

USS *George Washington*

Lying at rest alongside Pier 12 of Norfolk Navy Base in Virginia, the aircraft carrier USS *George Washington*, *GW* to her friends, makes an imposing but strangely beautiful sight.

Having undergone post-cruise refit, she looks brand new, spick and span, her gray paint-work fresh, gleaming, and clean as a whistle. A constant stream of sailors fuss industriously about her, seeing to her every need, her every whim, making those final preparations, those final checks.

This mighty warrior is poised in readiness. Soon, the USS *George Washington* (CVN-73), proud asset of the US Navy's Atlantic Fleet, will slip her lines and depart her home port of Norfolk. She will once again take to the high seas to do what these awesome warships, the biggest ever built, do best—project seaborne power.

Whether the *GW* is huge in size is a matter of comparisons. Although bigger than the biggest of ocean-going liners, there are in fact supertankers that exceed her dimensions, but

only in length. In all other proportions the mighty CVN is leader of the pack. However, size is relative, and as you approach her at Norfolk, the largest Navy base in the world, the *Washington*'s bulk seems diminished, swallowed by the vastness of her surroundings.

In the next pier, at berth alongside CVN-73 and separated by a mere 200 yards or so of water, is moored her elder sister, the venerable USS *Enterprise* (CVN-65), the first carrier constructed using nuclear propulsion and a vessel of some distinction. She was leading lady in the classic movie *Top Gun,* starring alongside Tom "Maverick" Cruise and Val "Iceman" Kilmer. But if that isn't enough to guarantee her everlasting fame, Captains James T. Kirk and Jean-Luc Picard have helped immortalize her name in the continuing voyages of the Starship *Enterprise*.

As one walks the length of the concrete promenade alongside the *GW*, an exercise that actually takes some minutes, the true size of these mighty towering CVNs becomes rather more apparent. High up on the carrier's flight deck, a sailor sweeps away the last vestiges of potential foreign object damage (FOD; debris that could be sucked into and damage the jet engines of the aircraft) from the brim of the immense flat-top. The diminutive human form helps lend a sense of scale, putting matters into truer perspective.

The GW's island superstructure is the only major blemish to the otherwise completely flat surface of the flight deck. The powerful crane in the foreground is intended primarily for use in removing aircraft damaged while landing. It can pick up a complete aircraft, quickly clearing it from the flight deck.

Ropes feed up to the USS Enterprise's *bow, while a couple of hundred yards away her younger sister ship, the USS* George Washington *prepares to once again return to sea. Norfolk Navy Base in Virginia, home to the US Navy's Atlantic Fleet, is where many of the giant aircraft carriers are to be found moored when not deployed at sea.*

Yes, the USS *George Washington* is big. She is, after all, home to 6,000 sailors and crew, give or take, and to 74 aircraft, although in an emergency she can accommodate up to 90. But let's be a little more precise. The *GW*'s vital statistics are 1,094 (feet, from stem to stern), 257 (feet, across the flight deck, her widest dimension) and 244 (feet, high from keel to mast tip), the latter equal to a 24-story building. All this metal work weighs in at a combat trim of 97,000 tons displacement.

RIGHT
The huge, permanently open void cut deep into the Washington's *flanks permits the transportation of aircraft from the hangar deck to the flight deck, via powerful elevators. In common with many of the US Navy carrier fleet, the mighty* George Washington *was built just a few miles away by the Newport News Shipbuilding Company. She was commissioned on 4 July 1992, after some 40 million man hours of labor, and at a cost of $4 billion.*

On the Washington's *hangar deck a sailor takes a moment to cast an admiring glance in the direction of sister ship* Enterprise.

Finally, the preparations are complete and the mighty CVN-73 leaves Norfolk, once again to roam the seas, policing the world's oceans and doing what these awesome warships do best—projecting seaborne military might. Dwarfed beneath the GW's bow, which towers some 65 feet up, the skipper of the tug Dekanawida feeds on the power, pushing and shoving, gently easing the giant carrier away from the pier. Four of these powerful little tugs shepherd the GW until she's clear of obstacles, at which time her own propulsion takes over.

Standing 65 feet proud of the waterline, the *George Washington*'s expansive flight deck resembles some massive, oversized gray football field. Indeed at 4½ acres it's certainly of sufficient area. Denuded of aircraft the giant armored deck engulfs you, seemingly going on forever. The *GW*'s resident air wing, Carrier Air Wing Seven (CVW-7) and its constituent squadrons will return to their roost later, flying aboard when she is once more at sea.

To the uninitiated the *Washington*'s flanks appear anything but streamlined. Angular protrusions jut from here and there that seem to have been added later, perhaps as an afterthought. In reality, of course, this is not the case; each metallic blemish to the carrier's otherwise svelte outer skin is there for a specific reason, for a purpose.

Most strange of all are the two enormous elongated voids severed deep into the ship's side. Measuring 60 feet by 20 feet, they permit external access to the *GW*'s cavernous hangar deck. Elevators, gigantic in both size and power, which in reality are moveable portions of the flight deck edge itself, use these cutaways to shuttle aircraft to and from the hangar bay and flight deck. The 3,880-square-foot elevators can hoist up to 130,000 pounds each, so a brace of Tomcats creates no problem at all.

The *George Washington*'s hangar bustles with activity as stores and supplies are ferried to and fro, deck hands utilizing numerous fork-lift trucks for the purpose, their task made rather

Meanwhile, at Naval Air Station Oceana, having conducted an exhaustive series of external checks, Lt. Chris "Basher" Blaschum of VF-143 climbs into the cockpit of his F-14 Tomcat. While the carrier was at Norfolk, her complement of eight squadrons and 74 aircraft were operating as usual, but from their "home" land bases scattered around the East Coast. Oceana is real Tomcat territory and frequently up to 100 examples of the jet can be found parked up on the ramp.

14

On CVN-73's bridge a young helmsman uses the small wooden ship's wheel to adopt the heading recommended by the 'gator. The small, diminutive wheel contrasts dramatically with the size of the ship that it steers. Nowadays, its function is electrical rather than mechanical, with very little effort being required to turn it. In the olden days, huge ship's wheels were required to overcome the physical forces involved in steering the rudder.

easier by the exclusion of aircraft. Once at sea, this enormous hangar space, measuring 850 feet in length by 140 feet in width, dimensions limited by the fact that it is encased within the ship's armored steel hull, will be brim full with neatly and efficiently parked rows of aircraft, their wings folded in contortions that marvel in ingenuity and mechanical ability.

The USS *George Washington*, like many of her sisters before her, was built by the Newport News Shipbuilding Company, whose dry docks

are situated just half a dozen miles away across the Hampton Roads, a stretch of water familiar to all outbound or homecoming CVs and CVNs. The *GW* was commissioned on 4 July 1992, six years after her keel had been laid, and after some 40 million man hours of labor had been expended on her construction.

The US Navy currently boasts 12 carriers in their inventory, these vessels split between two commands, the East Coast Atlantic Fleet and West Coast Pacific Fleet. Of these carriers,

Pride of place on the GW's bridge is reserved for the ship's commanding officer, Capt. Mal Branch. His suitably identified and elevated "barber's" chair is positioned on the port side of the bridge, in a location that allows the captain to monitor both the flight-deck action and the way ahead. Captain Branch will regularly confer with the 'gator, Commander Gerry Mauer over the ship's course, which during flight operations is a compromise between the carrier's own positional schedule and the air wing's requirements.

the *Independence, Kitty Hawk, Constellation,* and *John F. Kennedy* are CVs, powered by conventional oil-fired boilers. The newer CVNs, powered by nuclear reactors, are the *Enterprise, Nimitz, Dwight D. Eisenhower, Carl Vinson, Theodore Roosevelt, Abraham Lincoln, George Washington,* and the most recent family addition, the USS *John C. Stennis.* With the exception of the earlier *Enterprise,* all of these nuclear carriers are in the so-called Nimitz class, all virtually identical, encompassing only

small modernizations and improvements in design along the way.

For the future, the *Harry S. Truman* is scheduled for commissioning in 1998, followed around the year 2000 by the *Ronald Reagan.* These, in turn, will retire the aging carriers *Independence* and *Constellation.*

An aircraft carrier's statistics are immense, so it seems perhaps only appropriate that the cost of manufacture and operation of these floating cities is equally so. The construc-

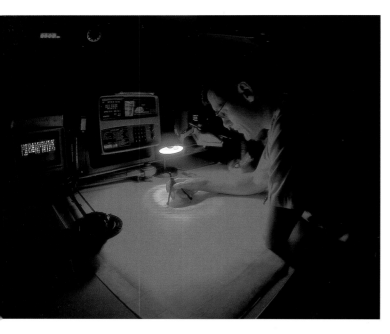

Although CVN-73 is equipped with all the very latest in highly accurate satellite navigation technology, it's kind of reassuring to see that the time-proven chart and brass dividers are still alive and well, linking the navigator's skilled profession with centuries of tradition. The job of 'gator, in keeping with all key positions aboard the carrier, is only open to those with carrier flight experience. However, in Commander Mauer's case it's with helos not jets, his logbook listing over 3,500 hours of flight time.

tion check for CVN-73 amounted to some $4 billion, a price that doesn't include her complement of aircraft, and her operating costs are in the region of $400 million per annum.

George Washington and her sister ships are powered by two nuclear reactors, a system that is considerably more efficient and versatile in operation than conventional oil-fired boilers. The net result however is the same—the production of steam, which (indirectly) turns the carrier's four 66,000-pound propellers at sufficient velocity to propel her 97,000-ton bulk at speeds well in excess of 30 knots (35 miles per hour).

In essence, a shipboard nuclear reactor consists of a quantity of uranium immersed in water. The resultant reaction is heat, and a lot of it. Indeed, the problem is in preventing it from spontaneously becoming too hot, a factor that is overcome by the insertion of "control rods." Since this process of fissioning also produces radiation, it is necessary to encase the reactors to protect the crew.

The by-product of all this heat is the generation of steam. In turn, the steam is used to drive both the turbine generators, which supply the ship with electricity, and the main propulsion turbines that power the massive 21-foot-diameter, five-bladed propellers, producing an available output of 280,000 shaft horsepower.

All personnel who come into contact with the *GW*'s reactors receive extensive specialist training in the theory and operation of nuclear power plants. Even the ship's captain had to undergo an intensive training schedule on the subject prior to taking command.

The installation of nuclear reactors permits a rather useful savings in both weight and space over the older oil-burning CVs. The conventional carriers have to make room for around 2 million gallons of fuel oil to burn in their eight or twelve boilers, this in addition to a similar quantity of aviation fuel for the aircraft.

Although hugely expensive to replenish when the time does come, this is in fact rarely necessary. The nuclear fuel entombed within a CVN's reactor will provide power for 15 years of continuous operation, together with a cruising range of some 1 million nautical miles. To equal such a distance, a conventional CV would have to burn a staggering 11 billion barrels of fuel oil.

Also eliminated is the necessity of taking on fuel for the nuclear carrier, although in reality a CVN is still obliged to restock her stores of JP-5 aviation fuel, as well as ammunition and other supplies. However, the reactor saves enough space to allow the carrier to hold 50 percent more jet fuel, a CVN's storage capacity topping some 4 million gallons, which decreases the

To remain operational while remote and at sea for long periods of time, it is essential that all but the most dramatic of maintenance can be conducted on board the carrier itself. This includes regular and remedial maintenance. In the jet engine shop, situated adjacent to the hangar bay, Aviation Machinist Mate Dwayne Berry puts the finishing touches to an F/A-18's General Electric F-404 engine.

frequency with which she needs to restock this essential commodity. When the carrier's stocks do run down, she can be supplied with fresh fuel and oil while still underway during an "unrep" or underway replenishment.

The mission of the USS *George Washington*, together with other similar carrier battle groups, is to provide mobile, flexible projection of tactical air power over both sea and land, and to effectively deter and dissuade potential aggressors. This objective is achieved through the *GW*'s eight embarked squadrons and their complement of 74 aircraft that constitute her assigned air wing, CVW-7.

In turn, the *George Washington* herself is assigned a supporting battle group together with a battle-group commander, an admiral, whose flagship she becomes. The composition of a carrier battle group may vary according to the deployment, the likely threat, and resources available. However, an operational battle-group task force will normally consist of 12 to 14 ships, including possibly a smaller antisubmarine warfare (ASW) helicopter carrier, and Aegis guided-missile cruisers. The latter mount sophisticated air-defense radars, anti-aircraft missiles, and Tomahawk cruise missiles.

In the main hangar, one of VA-34's old Intruders is given a cosmetic face lift, the wet paint on the panels that litter the deck is drying rapidly in the warm breeze that percolates through the bay. While sailing in warmer climates, the extensive hangar deck is a pleasant work environment, with plenty of light and fresh air, courtesy of the elevator access holes.

The principle function of this awesome combined task force is to protect the mother ship—the aircraft carrier herself, which due to sheer size and course predictability during flight operations, makes for a potentially vulnerable and inviting target.

But knowing and doing are two rather different things, and no potential aggressor will find a US Navy aircraft carrier easy meat. Her protective shield is both extensive and multilayered. Tactics are based on the concept

RIGHT
With 6,000 people on board, of whom many are involved in hard physical labor of a dangerous nature, the GW's extensive medical facilities are not just for show. Apart from an emergency room, operating theater, and many other facilities to be found in any well-appointed hospital, the Washington *is fitted with the Challenge Athena system, permitting x-rays and ECGs to be transmitted electronically back to the naval hospital at Portsmouth for expert analysis.*

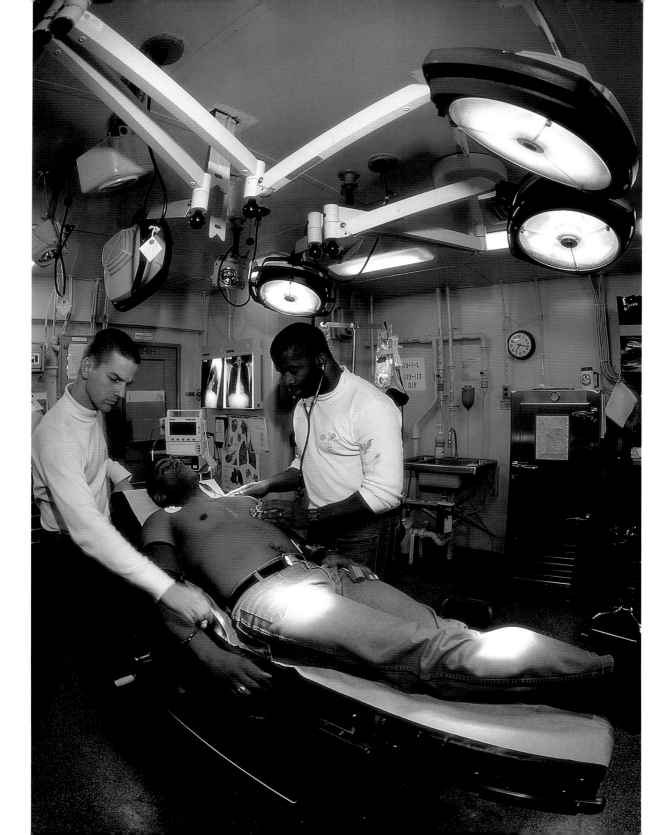

Feeding the 6,000 is an awesome task to undertake, but one that is accomplished with practiced aplomb by the crew who man the GW's massive galleys. Fresh bread is of course an important part of the sailors' diet and here a percentage of the carrier's daily output of 800 loaves is prepared for the ovens. Around 18,000 meals are served each and every day, that's breakfast, lunch, and dinner for each of the 6,000 crew members.

of defense in depth, beginning far, far out from the carrier, where ideally the threat—be it submarine, ship, or aircraft—will have been destroyed long before it is able to get within striking distance.

The battle-group commander, overseeing the action from the CVN's bridge or her combat direction center (CDC), will position his assets—subsurface, surface, and air—in such a manner as to provide maximum defense of the flagship.

If an aggressor were to break this outer shield, it would then be engaged by successive forces, by which time, in the rather unlikely event that it should reach the carrier, the threat's strength will have been diminished to such a degree as to make it vulnerable to the vessel's own close-in defensive systems.

Such last-ditch weaponry includes the Sea Sparrow medium-range surface-to-air missile, in addition to the awesome six-barreled Vulcan-

Once the food is prepared, it needs to be eaten in one of the large messing areas located throughout the ship. This is the chief petty officer's mess, which as the name implies, is reserved for that rank of personnel. The enlisted lower ranks have their own messing areas, while the 350 officers repair to the ward rooms, the lavishness of which would equal many high-class land-based restaurants. However, regardless of venue or rank of recipient, the food's always good—take my word for it!

23

Phalanx "Gatling" cannon, capable of firing 3,000 rounds of 20-millimeter ammunition per minute. Guided by dual radar beams and controlled by computer, the Phalanx's barrage is devastating and invariably deadly accurate.

In the meantime, while protected by this shield of force, the carrier's aircraft will be earning their keep. Her A-6 Intruders, although outdated and old-generation, can still pack a heavy punch when required, delivering their payload of high-tech guided weaponry to targets at ranges up to 500 miles. In the ground-pounding mission, the A-6 is supported in more than capable style by the newer-generation F/A-18 Hornet. But once this awesome twin-engined jet has performed its attack role, at the flick of a switch it can go defensive, redirecting its sting toward airborne adversaries, performing its dual role of fighter with superiority over most dedicated types.

The *GW*'s F-14 Tomcats, with their two-man crew, will fly combat air patrol (CAP), eliminating any airborne adversaries with their Phoenix missiles while still way beyond visual range. The million-dollar fire-and-forget Phoenix can lock on and kill a target at ranges up to 100 miles. In the meantime, EA-6B Prowlers wreak electronic havoc, turning the enemy's radar screens to snow, while the *GW*'s E-2 Hawkeyes, the carrier's "eyes in the sky," continue to track and confound the enemy. Scoping at ranges up to 250 miles, they provide the *Washington* and her airborne assets with the "big picture."

Illuminated by flat, dimensionless fluorescent lighting, the long passageways resemble a kind of hall of mirrors, with symmetrical knee-knockers receding into the distance. Frame numbers are painted onto the bulkheads, of which 260 span the ship laterally. Bull's-eyes giving more precise locational details are to be found frequently, but regardless, newcomers to this subterranean maze invariably lose their way.

To help keep the Washington's *complement up to speed on news and current affairs (as well as the latest offerings from Hollywood), the carrier has its own TV station,* GW Now. *Paul Jenkins and Tom Smith prepare to prerecord the day's bulletin for transmission later in the evening. The duo also have other daily tasks to perform and sometimes, when they conflict, the recording to airing times can get rather tight.*

The carrier battle group has the ability to bring a substantial force to bear, in relatively short order, anywhere in the world—anywhere that is within striking distance of the sea. The initiative is that just the presence of this incredibly powerful policing force will dissuade and discourage a would-be aggressor from actual physical conflict—ideally without launching an airplane in anger.

An example of this peacekeeping principle was exhibited in Iraq during 1994. In October of that year, Saddam Hussein decided to head south once again toward Kuwait. CVN-73 was duly dispatched to the Persian Gulf. At about the time she arrived on station, Saddam had second thoughts. Perhaps it was no coincidence that 80 percent of strike assets in theater were parked in Saddam's back yard, on the flight deck of the USS *George Washington*.

This also illustrates the changing role of the aircraft carrier in the changing world situation. The traditional "blue water" navy that once prepared to do battle on the high seas, mixing it with equally capable adversaries, is

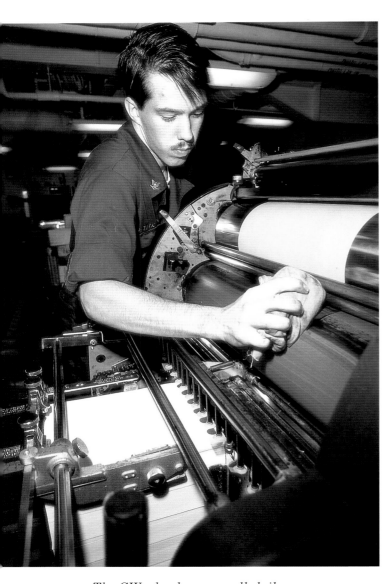

nowadays more prepared for localized conflicts that adjoin seas such as the Adriatic and Persian Gulf. The carrier has inherited the task of international peace-keeper, of international policeman.

The role of the aircraft carrier on the world's stage may have altered, but one element remains firmly unchanged: the role of the people, the ship's dedicated crew. Without them, a CVN could not operate and could no longer police the world's oceans.

The GW *also has a small daily newspaper produced in the print shop. In addition to the paper, all manner of other items are printed on board.*

Chapter Two

The Floating City

To make an aircraft carrier such as the *George Washington* work requires a vast amount of manpower. Although exact numbers vary from carrier to carrier and cruise to cruise, it takes around 6,000 men (and, in the case of an increasing number of carriers, women too) to make this complicated package work. Of the whole, some 2,500 men belong to the carrier's air wing, the remaining greater balance working the ship herself.

This statistic of human souls is one that at first is quite impossible to comprehend. Most "normal" ships such as destroyers and cruisers have a complement of around 400 men, an analogy being perhaps to a small rural village, its relative smallness permitting a more close-knit community. In contrast, the vastness of an aircraft carrier and her complement perhaps more resembles a larger town, with many of its inhabitants never meeting the bulk of the population, even perhaps their own neighbors, and only visiting the districts required for their own personal existence.

On the carrier, rarely are vast numbers of people visible. They're spread out, some on the

The enlisted men sleep in racks, rows of slim bunks stacked three deep. A narrow coffin locker beneath each rack provides a limited area for the storage of clothes and personal belongings, while small blue curtains draped around the bunk provide a degree of privacy.

flight deck, some the hangar deck, the remainder sprinkled at random throughout 2,500 compartments that divide the carrier into subterranean steel cubicles.

Each resident of this floating city has his own allotted task within. While the majority are involved directly in the operation of the carrier's aircraft or of the ship herself, many others perform vital jobs of a supportive, domestic nature to the community. Most of the amenities to be found in any small town are also present within the carrier. Some provide essential subsidence and support, while others are there to make life a little more bearable during the long periods at sea.

There's a bakery, a galley, a laundry, two barbershops, two convenience stores (known as "geedunks") that sell domestic products together with clothes and souvenirs, a chapel, a jail, a photo lab, a TV station that produces daily news bulletins, in addition to ensuring a regular flow of feature films, a radio station, newspaper, a library, a post office, a dentist, and the list goes on.

Physical fitness is encouraged, and the eight weight gyms positioned throughout the lower decks are rarely quiet. Thinking of everything, the US Navy generously provided the *GW* with a 4½ acre running area. If necessary, it can also be used for the launch and recovery of aircraft too! At sea, with the hot sun beating down and a refreshingly cool breeze blowing across the

In the ship's store, or "geedunk," a vast array of domestic goods are available, at highly competitive prices too. Particularly popular with souvenir-hungry visitors are the traditional brass Zippo lighters complete with engraved ship's badge, or the ubiquitous embroidered baseball caps.

Physical fitness is positively encouraged, and a number of small weight gyms are scattered about the decks. This one on 03 level is kitted out with both free weights and machines, ideal for a complete work out.

deck, the experience is welcome, particularly for those who spend most of their life below in the air-conditioned, artificially lit bowels of the ship.

In common with any self-contained community, a medical facility is an essential requirement. Manned by six doctors and a fully trained support staff, the *GW*'s medic center is equipped with an operating room, emergency room with full life support facility, laboratory, x-ray unit, hydrotherapy facility, and 67-bed inpatient, three-bed intensive-care and four-bed isolation wards. There's a pharmacy that stocks around 3,500 types of medicines and even has the capability to make eyeglasses. CVN-73's medic center is also equipped with the Challenge Athena sys-

tem, permitting the transmission of x-rays and electro-cardiograms (ECGs) back to the naval hospital at Portsmouth, Virginia, where specialists are on hand to provide expert diagnosis.

As with any "army" of men, the USS *George Washington*'s 6,000 complement march on their stomachs. They work long, hard hours, and three square meals per day are vital to keep energy levels up. The sheer enormousness of the carrier's catering requirement can perhaps be better understood with a few statistics. Each and every day while at sea, the staff within the *GW*'s huge, scrupulously clean galleys will prepare over 18,000 meals. The enlisted personnel consume theirs within huge mess

31

Unsurprisingly, the GW is equipped with its own meteorological department that supplies the ship and squadrons with up-to-date weather predictions. One means of gathering information is by balloon, an example of which is being launched from the stern of the carrier. The helium-inflated balloon will rise tens of thousands of feet, while a small sensor pack suspended from beneath relays data back to the meteorological office.

A group of sailors breath in the invigorating early morning air as they sweep the deck clean, brushing away a buildup of oil and grease that can make the surface very treacherous. The action also helps to remove potential FOD, including any small pieces of nonskid surface that can occasionally break loose.

rooms, while the officers enjoy a superior degree of luxury in their wardrooms. Regardless of where it is served, however, the food is invariably of high quality.

The *Washington*'s consumption of bread is such that some 800 loaves will be baked each day in vast ovens, her complement also managing to consume around 660 gallons of milk, over 2,000 eggs, and 500 pounds of hamburger meat. The strategically placed vending machines and dispensing fountains supply an equivalent of 13,000 cans of soda per day. Perhaps it's little wonder that satisfying the 6,000 sometimes seems an impossible task!

Below the armored flight deck and hidden from view within the carrier's outer skin is a veritable labyrinth of passageways and compartments, the complexity of which is guaranteed to confuse and confound all newcomers. The passageways head hither and thither, seemingly with no logical sequence, quickly ensuring all sense of direction will be lost.

Perhaps, however, salvation is at hand. Each compartment and each bulkhead has its own "bull's-eye"—code numbers stenciled in black upon a fluorescent yellow square. For those who can break the code, this sequence of letters and numbers identifies your precise location. For example: 01-170-5-L. The first digits (01) indicate deck or level, in this case one deck above the main or hangar deck. The hangar deck is numbered 1, those below 2, 3, 4, and so on, and those above 01, 02, 03, and so on.

The second set of digits in the sequence (170) indicates the frame number, of which 260 span the ship laterally. The foremost point is frame number 1, the aft-most frame 260.

At night, while many aircraft remain topside chained to the flight deck, others are brought down below into the hangar. During the hours of darkness the hangar space is only dimly illuminated by orangey sodium lighting.

From high up on vulture's row a sailor uses one of the large, powerful Aldis signal lamps to polish up his Morse-code technique. His silent conversation is with a counterpart aboard the Aegis guided-missile cruiser San Jacinto, *one of the* Washington's *support ships.*

The last figure (5) is the compartment number ranging from the centerline. Zero is on the centerline, even numbers to the port side (2, 4, 6), and odd numbers to starboard (1, 3, 5). Finally the letter (L) identifies the use of the area, which in this case is a living space.

Therefore 01-170-5-L is located one deck above the main (hangar) deck, at frame 170, which is about two-thirds down the ship and on the starboard side.

Armed with such precise information, surely it would be a matter of some ease to get around—but not so fast. As stated earlier, passageways are not always continuous, not always

logical. Furthermore, the near-vertical steel ladders that permit a change of level have a habit of hiding behind closed doors.

The newcomer's sense of confidence, gained of having successfully transited two or three levels unassisted, is as quickly snuffed when all further means of passage seems impossible. In bewilderment you search, for it must be here somewhere.

Finally, having wandered aimlessly, traversing further passageways that lead only to a state of total confusion, despair, and surrender, you resign to inquire of a passing sailor, who invariably points out the now only-too-obvious

Even though nuclear aircraft carriers such as CVN-73 can hold up to four million gallons of aviation fuel, during days of continuous flight ops this will need to be regularly topped off. However, this can be done underway during an unrep or underway replenishment. Here the USNS Big Horn, *one of the battle-group supply ships, transfers fuel across and into the GW's tanks.*

means of escape. Quickly, hiding embarrassment and frustration, you exit, but all confidence is lost.

Some longitudinal passageways stretch for what seems the entire length of the ship. As you look down the long corridor, it resembles a hall of mirrors, an illusion accentuated by the dimensionless, flat lighting and regular, uniform bulk-

heads. Every 20 feet or so is an arched steel bulkhead frame known as a knee-knocker. These identical openings appear to diminish in size, receding down the passageway. A person at the far end seems tiny, a reflection of oneself perhaps. You stride toward him in rhythmical fashion, six strides and then a step, hurdling the knee-knocker, six more and then another step, until finally, meeting in the middle, the passageway's narrowness demands that one person must give way to the other.

Crew with a little time to spare may tackle the long climb up to level 010 and "vulture's row." Beneath the plethora of radar antennas and other rotating electrical devices, a platform surrounds the "island," awarding a superb bird's-eye view of flight-deck activity. On a warm summer's evening there are few better places to be.

Nearby is the protruding gazebo of primary flight control or "pri-fly." Just below is the navigation bridge, the nerve center of the carrier, with rows of forward-facing green-tinted glass providing a grandstand view of the way ahead.

Pri-fly is home to the air boss, or more formally, the air operations officer. He has overall command and responsibility of all movements and operations on the flight deck and in the air up to 10 nautical miles in radius from the carrier. From pri-fly, the air boss and his deputy, the mini-boss, both former squadron commanders and veteran carrier flyers, control the launch, recovery, and flight patterns of all aircraft, ensuring that operations run smoothly, safely, and on time. The air boss's job is a very demanding one, his ability to make split-second decisions under extreme pressure a prerequisite. It takes a special kind of officer to nail the job down.

Meanwhile, on the bridge the captain surveys and monitors operations from his

A Vulcan-Phalanx six-barreled rotary cannon points threateningly from the stern of the carrier, ready to dispatch any unwanted visitors who manage to break through her outer defenses. Guided by radar and capable of firing up to 50 rounds of 20-millimeter ammunition per second, the Phalanx's deadly barrage rarely misses its target.

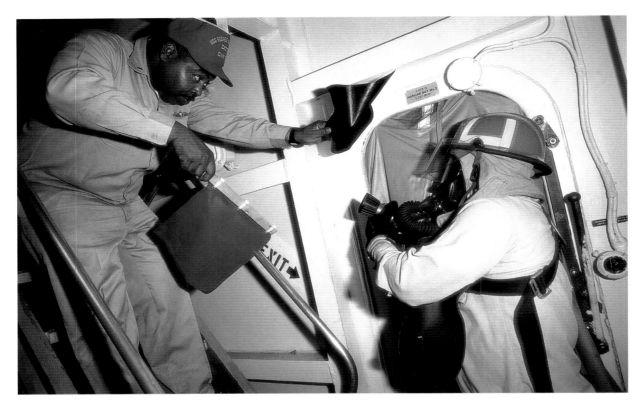

One of the principal dangers on any ship, and particularly on an aircraft carrier with its vast stocks of jet fuel, is that posed by fire. Consequently, the means to fight this is frequently practiced. Here, during one such training session, a sailor has been forced to reverse down a ladder by the evaluating chief petty officer. His red and black flags represent flames, and if one touches a firefighter, he's "dead." The act of backing down one of these steep ladders is difficult enough at the best of times and is made considerably more so when armed with a heavy hose.

lofty dark-blue swivel chair, which is situated on the port side, affording an excellent view of the flight deck. He will consult with both the carrier-air wing commander (called "CAG," a term left over from the days when the carrier's aircraft complement was called an air group) and the navigator (whose title is often shortened to 'gator), ensuring that the day's air plan and navigational commitments are executed.

In the center of the long and expansive bridge, a young helmsman steers the ship by means of a seemingly insignificant wooden wheel, it's smallness contrasting dramatically with the bigness of the vessel that it controls.

By tradition the captain of an aircraft carrier is a former carrier flyer with extensive previous command experience. The knowledge and understanding gained is vital, considering the purpose and role of the ship. It's generally recognized that the CVN captain's job is one of the most desired within the navy. With relatively few carriers in the inventory, there aren't many such positions available, and the select few who take command of a CVN are both very special and very fortunate.

Along with the captain and air boss, all key personnel such as the CAG, executive officer, mini boss, and 'gator wear naval aviators' "wings of gold," and usually have several thousand hours of flight experience.

The 'gator's task is one of the most responsible and pressured on the ship. With 97,000 tons of floating real estate under his direction, even a minor error can be both costly and highly visible. The 'gator works in conjunction with the captain and the CAG, ensuring that while the carrier's positional commitments are kept so also are the air wing's flight requirements met.

On a nuclear-powered carrier such as the *George Washington,* the 'gator's job is made a little easier, the ship's reaction to power command being instantaneous and therefore much more flexible in use. The older steam-powered CVs were slower to react and propulsion available depended on the situation of the boilers.

Nevertheless, a state-of-the-art CVN is still a big ship in a fluid ocean, and when maneuvering in tricky areas she can be a real handful. A carrier requires some 10 minutes to reverse direction and a fair distance to stop, factors that can easily magnify the results of the smallest error in judgment or mistake. Speed is often a balance between maneuverability—sufficient speed to provide enough wash over the rudders for positive directional control—and safety, 15 knots being a standard compromise in tight situations.

The key jobs such as captain, CAG, and 'gator are of course held by high-ranking officers with many years of service under their belts. In stark contrast, the average age of the flight-deck crew is just 19½.

During operations, the flight deck is an extremely dangerous location with many potentially lethal hazards just waiting to snare the unwary. The guys can be required to work very long hours, perhaps 16- or even 18-hour days. Their youth and fitness, combined with a healthy dose of enthusiasm, help them to stay alert and on top of the job for these lengths of time. Anyway, on an aircraft carrier there really isn't an awful lot to do in your spare time, so many live their work, taking a pride in their profession.

Eventually, when the enlisted men do knock-off, back at their berthing areas they'll perhaps watch a little TV or play a hand or two of cards before retiring for the night. The enlisted men's berthing consists of rows of narrow steel bunks known as "racks." Stacked three high, there maybe as many as 250 racks in one

The GW *also regularly practices general-quarters drill, in accordance with which gas masks must be worn should the simulated threat demand. However, this A-6 crewman takes such a mild inconvenience in his stride, his studies carrying on regardless.*

Although a rare occurrence it's a fact that crew do very occasionally go overboard. In such an eventuality, unless a helo is already airborne, in a matter of minutes this emergency rescue boat will be launched.

The multitiered steel superstructure of the island towers high above the flight deck. To the right on level 010, or vulture's row, is the small glass-fronted gazebo of primary flight control or pri-fly, from where the air boss controls all flight operations on and around the carrier. One deck below on 09 level is the navigation bridge and below that the admiral's bridge.

42

On fine-weather no-fly days a high percentage of the carrier's aircraft will be parked up on the flight deck. This concentration of perfectly "spotted" Hornets and Vikings occupy an area toward the bow on the port side termed "Four Row." The S-3 Viking's vertical tail plane is unusually high and consequently is designed to fold down horizontally prior to entering the hangar deck.

berthing area. A small curtain affords a modest degree of privacy, while a shallow "coffin locker" situated beneath the bunk is the extent of their personal storage space.

The flight crews and other officers are rather more fortunate. They have small staterooms that provide comparatively luxurious surroundings.

A brace of Tomcats await lifting from hangar to flight deck via elevator 3, situated aft of the island on the starboard side. These incredibly powerful elevators, of which there are four, one on the port side and three on the starboard, can uplift 130,000 pounds in one go.

44

Having just run up a Hornet's General Electric F-404 engines, a crew chief offers the traditional thumbs up—"She's good to go."

The size of the stateroom varies and may accommodate between two to eight men accordingly.

Equipped with wider, double-stack bunk beds and appointed with sink, locker, drawers, shelves, and writing desk, although still rather basic, the officers' accommodations are nevertheless actually quite comfortable.

Berthing spaces are situated at different levels within the hull of the ship, some immediately beneath the flight deck. During night ops, the crescendo of noise reverberating down from the steel deck defies belief. But oblivious, the tired, exhausted crews sleep soundly.

Meanwhile, a blueshirt tractor driver reverses an A-6 into its spot. Working under the command of the handler and yellowshirt flight-deck directors, the tractor driver's job is one demanding a high degree of skill, the aircraft being big and difficult to maneuver, especially at night, in the dark. A moment's lapse in concentration can easily result in expensive damage to an aircraft's vulnerable and delicate panels.

The aircraft must be parked precisely so that they can then be chained down in the most efficient manner. A yellowshirt plane director uses hand signals to command the final inches of movement so this F/A-18 is perfectly spotted. He wears a "Mickey Mouse" cranial helmet that incorporates a two-way radio set, with which he can communicate with the handler in flight-deck control.

The aircraft handling officer or handler controls all movement of aircraft both on the flight deck and the hangar deck. During air ops, the flight deck is both congested and constantly changing, and in flight-deck control, Lt. Jimmy McLaughlin, alias the handler (or "Mangler" as he's sometimes called), uses his weedgie board to plan the deck movements, ensuring all aircraft are where they should be to execute the air plan in the most efficient way. The use of suitably shaped and colored templates, although old technology, is still the best way to stay on top of the constantly evolving situation.

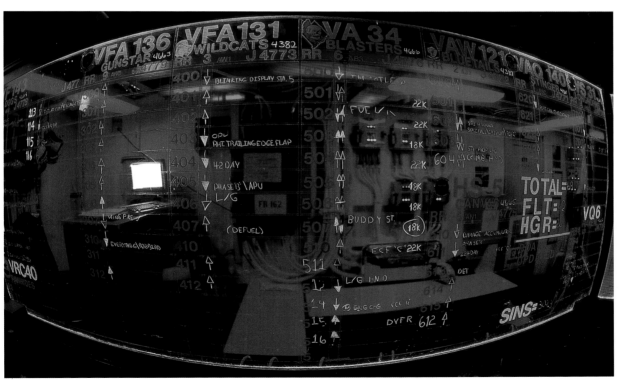

Mounted in front of the handler is the aircraft status board which is constantly updated with information about each aircraft on deck.

Chapter Three

The Air Wing

An aircraft carrier's entire reason for being is to project airborne power, and this is done through her embarked air wing. In the case of the USS *George Washington*, she provides a home to CVW-7.

A carrier air wing possesses an awesome capability to wreak havoc and destruction upon potential adversaries. By combining a number of squadrons, each dedicated or semidedicated to one specific mission, the resultant force is of undeniable ferocity and effectiveness. The squadrons work together in unison, complementing and supporting each other, and in common with all aspects of carrier operations, it's a real team effort.

CVW-7 employs some 2,200 people, of which about 280 are officers, mostly air crew. All of these folks are commanded by one man, the carrier air wing commander, an officer of vast experience, universally known as the CAG, a

The radiation warning symbol stenciled onto the nose of this EA-6B Prowler hints at the sinister equipment within. A modified version of the A-6 Intruder, the four-man-crew Prowler carries a plethora of electronic-countermeasures (ECM) equipment in underwing pods and in the aircraft's nose and tail capsule. The EA-6B's mission is to provide electronic protection to the carrier's strike force by detecting, confusing, and neutralizing the enemy's surveillance and guidance systems.

nickname reflecting earlier years when squadrons were formed into carrier air groups, as opposed to wings.

Typically, the CAG is of captain rank, possessing at least 20 years of experience as a naval aviator to call upon. Similarly to the post of carrier captain, the position of CAG is a much-sought-after billet, a successful tour doing the officer's career no end of good within the fiercely competitive, hierarchical naval structure.

On the *George Washington*, the captain of the ship and the CAG are equal, both in rank and status. The captain is in command of the CVN herself—in effect the air base—and all who work on and support her, while the CAG takes responsibility for the air wing, its aircraft, and its people.

At the time of this writing, CVW-7 comprises eight squadrons and 74 aircraft, the combination of which provides the flexibility to perform a wide variety of missions and taskings.

Ultimately, the primary function of the carrier and her battle group is to put ordnance onto targets, and this task is currently shared by two types of attack aircraft, the A-6E Intruder and the highly capable multirole F/A-18C Hornet.

The USS *George Washington* embarks just one squadron of A-6 Intruders, these flown by VA-34 "Blueblasters." The venerable old Grumman A-6 first saw active service with the fleet in

Similarly to racing cars and other means of high-performance travel, one error in the maintenance of a jet aircraft could spell disaster for its crew. The young, highly professional technicians are aware of the level of responsibility and are suitably precise and methodical in their work.

1963 and, having made its combat debut in Vietnam, has fought with distinction in every military action involving US Navy air power since.

By today's standards, the two-man crew (pilot plus bombardier/navigator) Intruder is a slow airplane, very much sub-sonic. Its mission was, and is, to deliver up to 15,000 pounds of bombs, either conventional or nuclear, against targets on sea and land, in all weathers, and by day or night. Nowadays, with the advent of "smart" precision-guided bombs, the Intruder is generally called upon to uplift considerably less in weight, one guided weapon doing the job more accurately and efficiently than a cluster of earlier "dumb" iron bombs.

Very much old technology, the Intruder is both slow and heavy to fly, being likened to a truck. Although perhaps a little unkind, this analogy is probably rather realistic. Nevertheless, over the years the A-6 has proved itself to be a reliable and effective weapons platform.

Currently, however, this old airplane is being phased out in favor of a new star of the show, the multirole F/A-18 Hornet strike fighter, of which the *GW* embarks two squadrons: VFA-131 "Wildcats" and VFA-136 "Knighthawks."

If the old A-6 can be likened to a Dodge truck, then surely the McDonnell-Douglas F/A-18 is a Dodge Viper. Incorporating state-of-the-art technology and with power in excess, courtesy of the two General Electric F404 afterburning engines, the Hornet is a pilot's airplane and a dream to fly. It is designed to minimize his in-cockpit workload, allowing the pilot to concentrate more fully on employing rather than actually flying the jet. Being multirole, such employment can either be "mud-moving" or pure white-scarf air combat maneuvering (ACM) or dogfighting.

In keeping with most current-technology fighters, the Hornet utilizes the hands-on throttle and stick (HOTAS) philosophy, designed so that most switches are situated either on the throttle or on the control column. This permits the pilot to rapidly change function or call up

A RIO examines the AIM-54 Phoenix missile slung beneath the wing of his F-14. The Tomcat is the only aircraft cleared to use this awesome radar-guided air-to-air missile, which can kill an adversary at up to 100 miles range. The heat-seeking Sidewinder missile above it is equally deadly, but at much shorter ranges.

data on his three multifunction displays (MFDs) or forward-facing head-up display (HUD), all at the movement of a finger and while "heads-up," looking out of the cockpit and maintaining situational awareness.

The Hornet also employs electronic fly-by-wire technology, meaning that in effect it is computer operated. When the pilot moves the stick, he is actually commanding the jet's on-board computer to initiate a maneuver. The computer instantaneously figures out the best means of

executing the command, often employing many of the aircraft's flight surfaces at once to perform outlandish maneuvers.

The F/A-18 is amazingly easy and stable to fly, a real bonus when it comes to getting the best carrier-arrested landing grades. At the flick of a switch, the jet can go from offensive to defensive, from dropping bombs on the enemy to mixing it up with his adversary's aircraft in the airborne arena. The Hornet does the job previously requiring two separate types of aircraft, a

A neat and orderly parade of F/A-18s, with tractor tow bars fitted, await the handler's pleasure. A crewman takes advantage of the down status of the flight deck to jog a few laps, hurdling the foot-snagging tow bars, arrestor cables, and other obstacles en route.

The steam-powered catapult's force is varied depending on the type of aircraft and its takeoff weight. The accuracy of the catapult system is important and is frequently checked by means of a gauge that measures its pull.

RIGHT
Frequently checked for broken strands or other signs of wear and tear are the arrestor cables. The cross-deck pendant, the section that is actually snagged by the aircraft's arrestor hook, takes the real strain and is therefore routinely replaced after 100 traps. The less stressed purchase cables are good for up to 2,000 arrestments, but their condition is regularly checked by eye.

byproduct of which is less aircraft and more room on the flight deck.

The Hornet can uplift a vast array of weaponry, the package mix depending on the principle mission to be flown. For pure air-defense work the '18 carries short-range AIM-9 Sidewinder missiles, together with medium-range AIM-7 Sparrows and the newer AIM-120 Advanced Medium Range Air-to-Air Missile (AMRAAM). The air-to-ground weaponry includes virtually every item listed in the US Navy inventory, including the AGM-62 Walleye electro-optically-guided bomb, AGM-65 Maverick air-to-surface guided missile, AGM-84 Har-poon anti-ship missile, AGM-88 High Speed Anti-Radiation (HARM) missile and Rockeye or BL-755 cluster-bomb units. For close-in defense or ground strafing, the Hornet is also equipped with the ubiquitous Vulcan M-61 20-millimeter "Gatling" cannon.

Although the F/A-18 can perform the air-defense role with enthusiasm, CVW-7's primary dogfighting capability is provided by the E-2C Hawkeye/F-14B Tomcat duo.

The *George Washington*'s E-2C Hawkeye squadron, VAW-121 "Bluetails," operates four examples of this twin-engined, turboprop-powered aircraft. Unmistakably identified by its dis-

A team of B-B stackers, or armourers, proudly display their shaven heads, posing in front of the suitably bald nose of an A-6.

One of the two armored bubbles in which the cat officer sits, and from where the catapults are fired. This bubble is responsible for shooting the two bow cats, while the other, situated amidships on the port-side deck edge, shoots the waist catapults. When the launch cycle is complete, the bubbles can be lowered down, a removable section of deck covering the remaining void.

tinctive 24-foot-diameter rotating radome, the Hawkeye is the carrier and the carrier battle group's eye in the sky, its mission airborne early warning (AEW) and command and control.

Normally during flight ops a Hawkeye, or "Hummer" as it is affectionately known, is first off the deck, its powerful radar and detection systems providing beyond-the-horizon targeting,

looking out to a distance of up to 250 miles. Nothing moves on sea, land, or air within a 3 million cubic mile surveillance envelope without the Hawkeye knowing about it.

To make this complicated, high-tech package work as advertised requires a crew of five—the pilot and copilot up front, and to the rear, ensconced within the cramped fuselage, an air con-

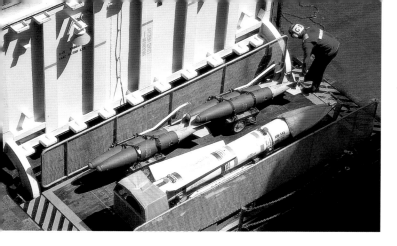

In addition to the four main deck-edge elevators that provide access to the hangar, other smaller versions permit the transfer of ordnance from the carrier's magazines several decks below. On this lift are four 250-pound dumb iron bombs, identified as inert practice examples by their blue paint, plus an AIM-54 Phoenix missile.

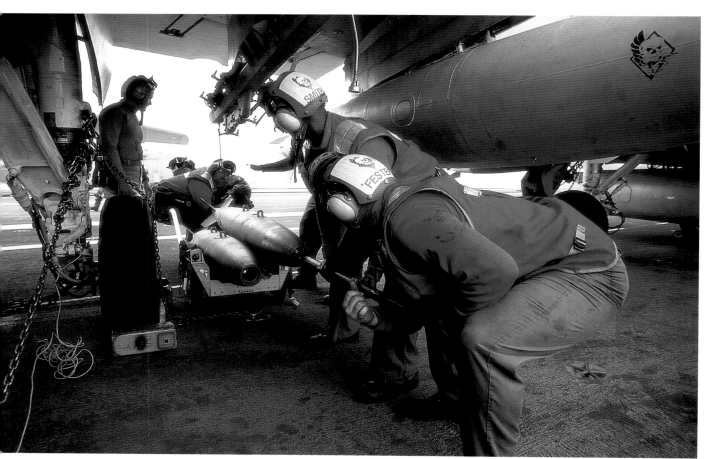

The B-B stackers, their bald pates now suitably protected by cranials, prepare to upload bombs onto an Intruder's racks. A removable steel rod temporarily screws into the bomb's nose, effectively increasing its length and permitting more men to help in the lift.

Up top on the flight deck, the jets are being prepared for their sorties. Meanwhile, one deck below on 03 level, the various squadrons are heavily involved in briefing their respective missions. Such a briefing may take as long as 90 minutes, planning in detail each facet of the sortie. Here, in the ready room of VF-143, the Tomcat crews take meticulous note of all relevant data.

trol officer, combat information center officer and radar officer. The information gathered is relayed back to the carrier's CDC and also directly to the F-14 Tomcats, which can then intercept, identify, and if necessary destroy any hostile targets.

The *GW*'s air wing currently employs one squadron of this immensely potent air-superior-

ity fighter, the Grumman F-14B Tomcat, operated by VF-143 "World Famous Dogs." Although the F-14 has been pounding the skies for a fair time, with uprated radar, avionics, and engines the Tomcat is still generally regarded as one of the most effective fighters in the air today. Equipped with the awesome long-range AIM-54

When the briefing is complete, it's time to put on all that cumbersome flight gear—g-suit, parachute harness, survival vest, and helmet—as ably demonstrated here by Hornet driver Lt. Jeff Lewis.

While the crews are below preparing for their sorties, back on the flight deck a multicolored wall of shirts slowly walks the length of the deck. All eyes are trained on the ground in this FOD walk-down, searching out the smallest piece of debris that could be sucked into a jet's air intake causing extensive and very expensive foreign object damage.

As the final preparations are made on deck to launch aircraft, the GW swings around into wind, a maneuver that is barely perceptible because of the carrier's bulk. Faithfully following in our wake, however, the San Jacinto leans out of the turn in a quite dramatic fashion.

Phoenix missile, the "Turkey" has the ability to "out kill" any other aircraft.

In addition to the Phoenix, the F-14 can still up-load conventional air-to-air weaponry such as the Sidewinder, Sparrow, and AMRAAM missiles. The Tomcat is also stealing some of the Hornet's thunder and developing a ground-attack ability, although nobody, not least the pilots who fly the jet, is in any doubt that the F-14 is a dogfighter. Perhaps there's a little of that fighter-pilot ego showing through here!

With a pair of General Electric F110 engines and auto-variable-geometry "swing-wings," the Tomcat outperforms most other aircraft, reaching a maximum speed of Mach 2.34 and a ceiling of some 60,000 feet. Nevertheless, although capable of high speed, with the wings swept fully forward to the 20 degree position, the F-14 is still very stable at slow speeds.

The work load within the Tomcat is shared between the pilot and his radar intercept officer (RIO). It is the RIO's job, as the name implies, to control and monitor the jet's radar and electronic systems, working independently or in conjunction with the E-2C Hawkeye to locate and track targets.

In today's world of high-tech warfare, it is essential that any airborne strike force is afforded a degree of protection by electronic countermeasures—a means of suppressing the enemy's radar and surveillance systems. Aboard CVN-73, this airborne electronic defense and warfare capability is provided by VAQ-140 "Patriots," who operate the EA-6B Prowler. Carrying a four-man crew, the Prowler is a modified version of the A-6 Intruder. However, instead of bombs, the EA-6 uplifts a plethora of electronic gadgetry that can turn the adversary's ground-to-air radar scopes to snow, neutralizing and effectively blinding them.

One of the major potential threats to the well being of a carrier battle group is that posed by the enemy's submarines. To counter this menace, *GW*'s air wing has a squadron of Lockheed S-3B Vikings flown by VS-31 "Topcats."

Now dressed in full hero gear, and with dark visor selected against the bright morning sun, Commander Pete Williams, skipper of VF-143, the "World Famous Dogs," prepares to strap on 60,000 pounds of awesome fighting machine, the F-14B Tomcat.

Strapped snugly into the jet, an F-14 pilot and his RIO are ready to spool up their F110 engines. Visible in the foreground, mounted on a wing pylon is an AIM-9 Sidewinder heat-seeking missile, designed to lock on and track its target's hot engine exhaust.

Initially, a subsurface threat needs to be located and identified, and for this purpose the Viking carries sonobuoys. Ejected from chutes beneath the aircraft's belly, these long, slim canisters descend under a drogue parachute and, on contact with the water, transmit sonar information back to the S-3. Once the sub is located, the Viking can then destroy it by use of depth charges and homing torpedoes.

Additional close-in antisubmarine warfare (ASW) capability is provided by the Sikorsky SH-60 Sea Hawk helicopters ("helos," in Navy parlance) flown by HS-5 "Nightdippers." The Sea Hawk, a navalized version of the Army's Blackhawk troop carrier, replaces the aging SH-3 Sea Kings. The Nightdippers' Sea Hawks also perform a search-and-rescue (SAR) mission, and there's always one in the air during launches and recoveries—a reassuring and comforting thought to many an air crew, no doubt.

Back on the fantail of the Washington, *the crew of a VF-143 Tomcat perform their final preflight checks to engines, avionics, and weapons systems.*

A brownshirt plane captain shoulders the chains recently removed from an A-6 Intruder as he supervises the aircraft's starting procedure. The jet's serviceability is his responsibility, and as a consequence, he monitors its preflight run up with a high degree of interest.

Raised voices are the order of the day in defiance of the crescendo of noise that now pervades the flight deck. Here, an F/A-18 driver attempts to communicate a message to a member of his support crew.

With wings swept fully aft this F-14 seems crouched, it's shoulders hunched and coiled ready to pounce, like some wild (Tom)cat that must be lashed down.

Chapter Four

Flight Deck

Early in the morning, the sight that greets the flight-deck hands is one that is no longer new to them. Running alongside the USS *George Washington*, connected by several cables and pipes is the rather smaller bulk of the supply ship USNS *Big Horn*.

Aviation fuel is the principal commodity being transferred during this unrep (underway replenishment), hundreds of thousands of gallons of the stuff. It's a spectacle that the majority of *GW*'s youthful but highly professional crew have seen many times before. Following a brief glance they dismiss the action and carry on with their duties, regardless.

Today's air-plan will commence at 1200 hours—on the button if the air boss gets his way, flight operations continuing well into the following night. The day's flight schedule will have been meticulously choreographed the previous evening by the air wing operations staff. The CAG, operations officer (opso), and squadron commanders each have their say, putting forward their own needs and requirements. The resultant air plan should largely

Viewed from vulture's row, an S-3 Viking proceeds onto cat one, the starboard bow catapult, while a Hornet and Prowler are transferred from the hangar to flight deck via elevator two.

satisfy all parties concerned. Copies are dispatched to relevant personnel including the captain, air boss, and handler.

The handler's, or more correctly the aircraft handling officer's, job is to orchestrate all aircraft movements on the flight and hangar decks and to coordinate the maintenance activities, arming, and refueling requirements of the squadrons. Working closely with the air boss, the handler must ensure that aircraft are suitably prepared and positioned on the deck, to coincide with and execute the day's air plan in the most efficient manner.

Situated in the superstructure or "island" at flight deck level is flight deck control, the handler's headquarters. Here the handler and his team sit around an eight-foot mock-up of the flight deck known as the aircraft spotting board or "weedgie board." Each aircraft is represented on the board by a miniature, shaped and colored template that is moved to precisely mimic and simulate actual movements on deck.

Diagonal stripes identify jets that are "down" or unserviceable, the addition of colored pins, wing-nuts, and similar hardware signifying aircraft that need fueling or arming. Using the weedgie board, aircraft movements can be rehearsed prior to actually executing them on the cramped flight deck. Although low-tech, the weedgie board provides an excellent overview of deck status.

Dedicated aircraft maintenance crews have worked late into the previous night ensuring that jets required are on line. Minor maintenance is often conducted on the flight deck, aircraft that require more extensive work descending, via one of the four huge elevators, down below to the hangar.

By now, however, the majority of maintenance work is complete, and aircraft are being respotted in accordance with the handler's directions. There are currently some 45 aircraft on deck, many of which are parked forward, on the bow. Towed by small tractors, these are now removed, some being deposited in front of the island on the starboard side of the ship, while others, principally F-14s and F/A-18 go to the stern, or fantail. In accordance with the handler and his weedgie board, each jet will be positioned so that when the time comes they can be taxied to their assigned catapults in the correct order, with the minimum of fuss and time loss.

The men working the deck wear "cranials," shell-like helmets incorporating ear protection and goggles. Some cranials are fitted with a two-way radio head-set called a "mouse,"

From up in pri-fly, Captain Pat Twomey, the air boss, or more formally air officer, has overall control and responsibility for all movements on the flight deck and in the air around the carrier. Carrier-based flight operations are a very time-critical evolution, and it's the air boss's job to ensure that the daily air plan is executed safely and on schedule.

Not unnaturally, a carrier is equipped with all the air-traffic-control facilities normally found on any land-based airport. The CATCC houses an array of radar screens, displays, and status boards, necessary to monitor and command all airborne movements.

which allows communication with the air boss, handler, and flight-deck officers. Most, however, don't have this luxury, and for them, the primary means of communication on deck is by hand signal. Over the years, a comprehensive flight-deck semaphore language has been compiled.

The deck work force also wears various brightly colored jerseys and "float-coats," the latter a survival vest equipped with floatation bladder, beacon, marker dye, and a whis-tle, useful if you're blown overboard. It does occasionally happen.

The color of the individual's polo-neck "shirt" also provides a strong clue as to his function on deck. The most visible are the "yellow-shirts," and appropriately, it is they who control the flight deck. The handler wears a yellow shirt, as does the air boss, flight-deck officer, flight-deck chief, catapult and arrestor-gear officers, and the plane directors.

An E-2C Hawkeye from VAW-121 backtracks the deck en route to one of the waist catapults situated abeam the island. It's general policy to launch a Hawkeye first, and with their distinctive rotating radome, there's always one somewhere up there during flight ops, providing airborne early warning and command and control. They're effectively the carrier's "eye in the sky."

The flight-deck officer directs and oversees operations on deck, while the chief "calls the deck" and is always visible in the thick of the action, his junior plane directors walking with and guiding the aircraft as they taxi. The yellowshirts are at the top of the flight-deck hierarchical pile. They call the shots.

Blueshirts are chock-and-chain men. As soon as an aircraft parks up on deck it's their responsibility to ensure that it is securely chocked and, if necessary, chained down. For this purpose the flight-deck surface is liberally sprinkled with spot points where sets of chains can be attached. Blueshirts also operate the tractors and "huffers," the aircraft starting units.

Redshirts are the flight-deck fire department, responsible for both fire fighting and crash rescue. However, a redshirt with black stripe indicates a "B-B stacker," an ordnance man. He

An A-6 prepares for launch off of one waist cat as an antisubmarine warfare Viking taxis toward the other.

and his brothers prepare and upload the bombs onto their racks, the missiles onto their pylons. They also operate the mechanical loader for the Tomcat's and Hornet's M-61 Gatling gun.

Greenshirts operate the catapult and arrestor gear, hooking up aircraft to the catapult and preparing it for launch, as well as looking after the arrestor cables. Purpleshirts handle the "motion lotion," fueling and defueling the aircraft.

Brownshirts are the plane captains. It's their responsibility to ensure that aircraft are inspected and serviced prior to flight and generally are in clean, sound condition. Last, the whiteshirts belong to those involved with safety factors. The LSO or landing signal officer wears a white shirt.

While the "shirts" are energetically preparing the aircraft and the deck in readiness for today's scheduled events, below in the vari-

Whiteshirt troubleshooters attached to VAW-121 "Bluetails" provide a final last chance check of the Hawkeye before it is catapulted down the deck.

ous squadron ready rooms, preflight briefings are well and truly underway. The pilots and crews spend some considerable time preparing for each and every "hop," briefing the mission in fine detail and outlining any conceivable eventuality. Each 90-minute flight may require a similar duration in both prebrief and postflight debrief, essential if the maximum amount of knowledge and learning is to be gleaned from every valuable training sortie.

Meanwhile, as the first air crews start to don their flight kit, a multicolored wall of shirts walks the deck from bow to stern. All eyes are focused upon the nonskid surface during the slow FOD walk-down, searching out the smallest nut, bolt, or piece of wire, which could so easily be sucked into an air intake, causing expensive damage to a delicate jet engine.

As the walk-down party disperse, their job done, the first air crews emerge from the island's steel hatch. Now dressed in full "hero" gear—G-suit, survival vest, parachute harness, and helmet with dark visors selected in defiance of the bright morning sun—they stride purposefully toward the waiting aircraft.

At the Tomcats of VF-143 "Dogs," parked way aft on the GW's fantail, the first crew reach their charge. While the RIO clambers up the steps and settles into the rear cockpit, busying himself with the switchology for flight, his pilot performs a detailed preflight walk-around, checking and inspecting the big jet for anything that's perhaps not quite right.

The redshirts have loaded Phoenix and Sidewinder missiles onto the pylons, the security of which the pilot tests with a reassuringly hefty shove.

Meanwhile in the "Corral," the name given to the area forward of the island on the starboard side, similar treatment is being awarded to a quintet of A-6 Intruders. Suspended from their wing-mounted racks are curious miniature blue practice bombs. About two feet in length, they're designed to accurately simulate the trajectory of their larger full-size cousins, but at considerably reduced cost to the taxpayer. A blank cartridge located in the nose provides both flash and smoke evidence of the bomb's impact point.

By now, engines are being fired up all around, and the decibel level has risen dramatically as a consequence. A glance toward the horizon reveals that we are rapidly altering course, deviating from that recommended by the 'gator, coming around into the wind. The GW's bow wave traces a smooth curving arc off the port side. The carrier is so big, so massive, that were it not for visual clues our maneuver would have been quite imperceptible, unlike aboard the

Aegis guided-missile cruiser USS *San Jacinto*. She follows faithfully in our wake but leans out of the turn at an alarmingly dramatic angle.

It's around 1145 hours when the first aircraft are untethered, and while the blueshirts scuttle away to stow the now-redundant chains, the plane directors use hand signals to marshal the jets to their waiting catapults. By now the deck is a hostile, noisy, and more important, very dangerous place to be. All around, jet engine air intakes wait to devour the careless or, alternatively, at the other end, blow a frail human body high into the air as if it were just a rag doll.

The massive propellers of the E-2 Hawkeye slash and cut as it proceeds to the left waist catapult. The Bluetails' "eye in the sky" will be one of the first to be shot into the blue yonder. Already airborne is a Sea Hawk helo, which will hold off, waiting and watching, just in case its lifesaving SAR duties are required.

A yellowshirt plane director guides and coaxes the twin-engined Hummer toward the cat, the shuttle of which interlocks with the tow bar attached to the nose-wheel leg of the aircraft. Within seconds the Hawkeye is gone, tell-tale wisps of steam emanating from the cat track the only evidence of its passing. On the stroke of 12—that'll keep the air boss up in pri-fly happy.

Already, the next aircraft is taxiing forward to take its turn in the launch sequence, this time an F/A-18. Once again, using only visual clues, the yellowshirt quickly but skillfully guides the Hornet toward the cat track. Exact alignment is crucial. As he makes the final minute adjustments the catapult shuttle is rapidly retracting back down the track from the previous launch. Cylindrical fittings on the nose tow bar engaged into the front of the shuttle, the only portion of the massive steam-driven catapult system that actually protrudes above deck.

Thunder fills the air and the deck shudders as a jet comes to full power up forward on

The cat officer located in the centrally positioned bow bubble awaits some business as the greenshirt cat and arrestor-gear men prepare the catapult to accept another airplane. Meanwhile, the deck trembles, as in the background an F/A-18 Hornet is launched off one of the waist cats.

one of the bow cats. Seconds later the roar diminishes as an A-6 is accelerated down the deck and off the bow of the ship. As the bomber struggles into the air, back at the waist cat, a greenshirt hook-up man gives the nose-tow-bar union a sharp whack with the heel of his boot to ensure conformity. Meanwhile, a second removable bar is connected aft of the nose wheel. This is the hold-back device, designed to literally hold back the aircraft under extreme force, and only give way when a predetermined load is attained. Precisely machined, hourglass-shaped, breakable metal hold-backs are used for all aircraft types except the F/A-18 and F-14. A "repeatable-

release" hydraulic hold-back device is used in the launch of these fighters.

To the rear of the Hornet, a huge moveable portion of the flight deck rears upward—the JBD or jet-blast deflector—while to the side a shirt holds aloft a board on which the aircraft's weight is written. The pilot offers a thumbs up in return, acknowledging and verifying the figures to be accurate. The steam-powered catapult will be set according to this weight, and it must be correct. If the power dialed in is insufficient the "cat stroke" will be weak, possibly depositing the unfortunate aircraft off the bow and into the drink. Too much power, at best will give the

The hook-up man gestures for an F/A-18 to creep slowly forward so that its nose tow bar will slot into a detent in the front of the cat shuttle. The hydraulic repeatable-release hold-back device has already been connected and will be locked into position to the rear of the jet's nose wheel. Out of sight below the jet's nose, the hook-up man's instructions are relayed to the pilot by the cat officer at deck edge.

recipient pilot the ride of his life, and at worst, could damage the aircraft structurally.

Once both the nose tow and hold-back bars are secured, the cat is tensioned to a preset value of around 4,000 pounds of pressure, so the nose wheel is now pinioned in a tug-of-war between the pull of the shuttle and the restraint of the hold-back.

The hook-up man, satisfied that his job is done, gives a winding motion with his hand and then points forward, at which signal the yellow-shirt plane director standing in view of the pilot gestures for "brakes off, full power!"

The hi-tech F/A-18's launch cycle is automatic and, having set the computerized flight control system, the pilot is now just along for the ride. Or at least until the jet is launched off the bow of the ship, when he will regain control. The pilot prepares for the big shove, head back against the ejection seat, gloved fingers gripping handles to the left and to the right of the canopy frame.

The jet's afterburners glow, and the deck trembles and shakes in response to the restrained force; the jet's rapid forward progress halted only by the hold-back device.

Quickly the hook-up man springs clear; in so doing, he hands the jet off to the cat officer. Shirts positioned down the left and right of the

Hornet give it a rapid "last chance" check, finally offering a thumbs up. At the same time, the pilot scans his instruments for any signs of problems. Should any now arise he will cry "suspend, suspend, suspend," canceling the shot. But everything seems fine, and the pilot snaps a salute toward the cat officer, signaling his readiness. The blue touch paper is now well and truly alight on this explosive situation.

The cat officer crouches low, takes one last look to check the jet's path and touches the flight deck with his hand. He then points one arm with two fingers extended down the deck, at which

final signal the "shooter" ensconced in the armored "bubble" (there are two of these small glass-paneled gazebos, one for the waist cats and one for the bow cats) depresses the firing button to shoot the cat.

Almost instantaneously the catapult reaches its preselected full pressure. The holdback finally gives way to the undeniable force, and the Hornet is propelled forward—0 to 150 miles per hour in 310 feet and just two seconds.

Even before the jet leaves the deck, which it does with a *thunk* audible throughout the entire ship, the JBD is dropping back down flush with the deck. The next jet is taxiing forward, and the well-rehearsed launch process is beginning once again, the whole scenario taking considerably less time than it does to read this description of it.

The force imposed by the catapult stroke imparts an acceleration of some five to six times the acceleration of gravity (G), enough as one pilot describes it "to fold the world around your ears." The sense of deceleration when the shuttle finally releases is also quite dramatic. For all the world it feels like you have stopped.

While day cat shots could perhaps be described as exhilarating, turn out the lights and it's a whole different situation; a night cat shot can be very scary indeed. You're blasted off into the darkness, into a black void that, with no exterior attitude reference, can be both confusing and disorienting. Pilots have gone off the bow with every sense in their body telling them they're 90 degrees wing down and only seconds from a watery grave. A glance at the instruments contradicts your body's screams, telling that all is fine, all is well. Nevertheless, it still takes every ounce of willpower to trust those dials, to ignore the urgent instructions your body gives you.

The *George Washington* is equipped with four steam-powered catapults—two forward on the bow and two amidships in the waist. Essentially, the catapult comprises two 315-foot-long cylinders or barrels situated just below the flight deck, one to each side of the track. Within each barrel is housed a large piston, the two of which are centrally connected by the shuttle. In essence, the catapult resembles a kind of enormous double-barreled shotgun.

When ready to shoot, steam is admitted through variable launch valves into the barrels,

Once the aircraft have taxied into position on the catapults, huge moveable sections of the deck rear up behind them. These are the JBDs, angled so that the jet's hot exhaust is directed skyward.

forcing the pistons forward. The amount of steam admitted, and therefore force generated, is dependent upon the weight and type of aircraft. The launch valve is normally set to give flying speed plus 15 knots. On completion of the cat stroke, the pistons' forward velocity is halted by a water brake, which incredibly, considering the forces involved, stops them within a mere three to five inches of liquid.

Flight operations from aircraft carriers are different from land-based operations in that they are cyclic and a very time-critical evolution. Whereas an air force wing may release flights of jets pretty much at will, a carrier is less flexible and more precise. The average cycle duration, involving perhaps 14 or 15 aircraft, is one plus 30, meaning time of launch to initiation of recovery is 90 minutes. After the first cycle is dispatched, which takes around 10 minutes to accomplish, the second cycle will launch 80 minutes later, followed immediately by recovery of the first wave.

If for any reason the launch is delayed or extended in duration, this in turn will mean that the following recovery will also be delayed and extended. Meanwhile, the returning aircraft holding overhead are burning into their possibly already low fuel reserves. On an aircraft carrier, it is therefore critical to both launch and recover aircraft on schedule, on time.

From the same cat a Prowler is launched off the bow of the Washington. *The JBD is already dropping down, following which, and without delay, the waiting Hornet will be directed forward onto the cat track. The launch is a very critical time, particularly for relatively low-powered, but possible highly loaded aircraft such as the A-6. If the cat stroke should be weak, with insufficient power, the jet would be in danger of being dumped off the bow and into the water. If the aircraft has not achieved a predetermined air speed on crossing the bow, the crew will immediately eject.*

Wisps of steam escape from the cat track as a yellowshirt plane director guides an F/A-18 forward onto the catapult. Perfect line-up is critical, and as with all facets of the launch, the pilot relies heavily on the judgment and professionalism of the young guys who work the deck, the average age of which is just 19½. To the left, a greenshirt holds aloft a board on which the aircraft's launch weight is indicated, in this case 45,000 pounds. Once the pilot has confirmed this figure to be correct the catapult will be set accordingly, so that it provides the perfect amount of acceleration off the deck.

As soon as the launch and recovery cycles are completed, the ship can then turn out of wind, going back onto its preferred course and also becoming less rigid, less predictable. A typical peacetime flying day will consist of eight cycles throughout a 12-hour period. However, in extreme combat situations, flight ops can be per-formed around the clock, crews working an 18-hour day, sleeping for six.

One of the principle feats that separates naval aviators from all others is the act of land-ing back on the ship. Instead of having the luxu-ry of a stretch of concrete thousands of feet long, a Navy pilot must accurately target his jet into a

Finally, the cat reaches full power, adding this to the thrust of the aircraft's own engines, the hold-back gives way, and an F-14 blasts forward—0 to 150 miles per hour in two seconds and 310 feet. To the left of the accelerating Tomcat is the waist bubble from where the catapult has just been fired, and forward of the bubble is the LLD or meatball.

nest of cables covering an area of just 120 feet, often at night and in the weather. Careers can be made or broken depending on how well a pilot "flies the ship," and there's a lot of visibility and pressure involved. Also a lot of pride.

Under the direction of the carrier air traffic control center (CATCC), aircraft returning from their sorties will orbit the ship at predesignated altitudes—Hornets at 2,000 feet, Tomcats and Prowlers at 3,000 feet, Intruders at 4,000 feet, and Hawkeyes and Vikings at 5,000 feet. From their five-mile orbiting patterns, the pilots will "hawk the deck," watching and waiting for their turn to join the landing circuit.

When it's time, the jets descend, usually in groups of two or three, joining the carrier's 800-foot circuit on the "dead" starboard side. They fly parallel with the ship, going into a hard left break over the top, pulling perhaps six G to make the maneuver look good and snappy—after all, you never know who might be watching! The jets make a staggered break, introducing a gap of around 45 seconds, the ideal approach separation, which, if everything goes well, will provide just enough time for the previous "trapped" aircraft to be cleared safe of the flight deck's foul line, and the arrestor cable to be reset.

The carrier's deck is equipped with four transverse-mounted arrestor cables or "wires" for the recovery of aircraft, each of which has its own engine below the deck. Just as knowing the weight of the aircraft was critical during the launch cycle, it is equally so for the recovery. The crewmen who operate the arresting-gear engines dial in the weight of the aircraft, which in turn adjusts the resistance incurred. The heavier the jet, the greater the resistance.

The carrier's circuit is tight, its final approach leg short. As soon as the pilot turns onto final and is in line with the deck, he'll be looking for the "meatball," the light landing device (LLD). Situated midway along the left edge of the deck, the LLD is an ingenious collection of lights, the path of which, if followed with

Another Tomcat launched from the inboard waist catapult climbs away from the deck, curving to the left as it does so to avoid conflicting with any aircraft that may be launched simultaneously off one of the bow cats.

required accuracy, will bring the airplane down at exactly the correct point on the deck.

The LLD consists of a row of horizontal green datum lights running centrally, within which is a vertical stack of five amber Fresnel lenses. The position and angle of the amber lenses is such that only a small "ball" of light can be seen at any one time, the placement of which within the vertical line depends on the viewing angle of the pilot's approach. Ideally, he will fly his aircraft in such a manner as to bracket the amber "meatball" centrally between the left and right rows of green datum lights. If his approach

The LLD or "meatball" is designed to provide an approaching aircraft with a visual reference as to the correct glide slope. Accurately followed, it'll bring a jet onto the deck for a perfect three-wire trap. Running centrally are five vertically mounted amber Fresnel source lights—the meatball itself. Only one of these, or a proportion of one, appears lit at any given time, making an amber ball, the perceived height of which depends on angle of approach. Mounted horizontally across are 14 (seven each side) green datum lights to align the ball with. The four red vertical lights positioned on each side of the ball are the wave-off lights, which can be illuminated by the LSO to wave-off (or overshoot) an approaching aircraft should the deck be fouled or his glide slope too erratic.

is too high, he'll see the amber ball above the green datum, the amount of vertical displacement dependent on the degree of deviation from the ideal glide slope. Conversely, if he sees a low ball, he's below the optimum path.

The closer you get to the LLD the more accurate its reference becomes and the more fine the control inputs required. In effect, the pilot actually flies down an invisible "cone" of error. Way out, and with the ball nicely centered, you could still be perhaps 20 feet out vertically. But as you follow the meatball in, the cone gradually reduces in size, guiding your descent until finally, on touch down, the margin of error has reduced to only a couple of feet or so. A really skilled "ball-flyer" can "crest the ball." He uses fine and precise inputs of power to keep him at the top, safer edge of this invisible cone, flying the ball down to the deck to catch a perfect three wire.

The aircraft carrier is equipped with four arresting cables or "wires" that span the flight deck, each some 40 feet apart. An approaching aircraft's tail hook will ideally impact the deck smack in the center of the cluster, midway

A cry of "fouled deck" prompts the LSO and his deputy to hold their pickle switches aloft, the effort a reminder that the flight deck is currently unclear to accept an aircraft for landing. If the deck remains fouled, he'll depress the button on his switch, illuminating the wave off lights on the LLD, commanding the approaching pilot to overshoot. He also holds a phone by which he can verbally communicate with the pilot. Sometimes referred to as "Paddles," the LSO is the descendant of that brave fellow who, on the wooden-decked carriers of World War II, used to guide in the piston-engined fighters using "table tennis" paddles.

between the second and third wires, so that it then runs forward, catching the third.

Because it is the pilot's eye that actually follows the ball, and as the distance between tail hook and eye varies between aircraft types, so the LLD can be tilted to compensate. The hook-to-eye distance of an F-14 is, for instance, considerably greater than for a smaller A-6. If the Intruder pilot flew the same line as the Tomcat, his hook would actually be too high, hitting the deck long, forward of all four arresting cables.

Conversely, and more dangerously, if a Tomcat driver flew the same line as an Intruder, he'd follow a low glide-path and, with a degree of error thrown in, would be in peril of colliding with the "ramp," or stern of the ship. Therefore, the LLD is tilted so that, although the pilot's eye may follow a different path, the all important tail hook will actually touch down at exactly the same point, between those two wires—the second and third.

The angle of the ball is adjusted for each approach by the LSO, a veteran naval aviator, highly experienced in the mystic art of the carrier landing. In company with two or three junior LSOs and a similar number of assistants, he has a privileged view of events, standing on a small platform at flight-deck level situated on the aft port side of the ship.

The LSO's ancestor during World War II was that brave fellow who, armed only with a pair of brightly painted "table tennis" paddles, employed semaphore to guide in the Hellcats, Wildcats, and Corsairs. The nickname of "Paddles" has stuck to this day, and although electronics have replaced the use of paddles, the LSO still performs a vital function in getting the aircraft safely back aboard the ship.

Paddles watches intently as the first jet to recover, an F/A-18 Hornet, curves around to pick up the glide slope. The pilot "calls the ball" at three quarters of a mile range—"405 Hornet, ball, 50"—which translates to the tail number of the jet, type of aircraft, confirmation that the pilot has visually acquired the LLD, and fuel remaining, in this case 5,000 pounds.

"Roger ball," the LSO responds.

Ordinarily, if the approach is good, the LSO will need to say nothing more, the pilot using his own skill and adjustment together with the meatball to bring the jet onto the deck. However, if the line-up is not good, the LSO will start to give advisory calls such as, "Don't settle; a little power; come left."

It's very important for an aircraft to correct its line-up early and get established "in the groove" at distance from the carrier. A good LSO will vary his voice tone dependent on the urgency and degree of reaction required. Early advisory calls will be controlled and calm. However, if an out-of-shape pilot chooses to ignore these, the closer the aircraft gets to the deck, the more urgent and forceful will be the LSO's commands.

His skill is absolutely amazing. Using his eyes to visually judge an aircraft's glide slope and ears to determine its power setting, the LSO can quite literally talk, or "lip-lock" an aircraft onto a heaving deck. If things do go wrong, the LSO has the authority to command him to go around, using his "pickle switch" to illuminate a cluster of red lights surrounding the meatball to "wave off" the aircraft.

But Hornet 405 needs no such assistance or command from Paddles, who pivots round on his heels to watch as the fighter flashes past, impacting the deck with a *thunk*. The F/A-18's tail hook instantly grabs the three wire, earning the pilot an "OK three" pass in the LSO's notebook. He grades and critiques each carrier landing , the results of which are indicated by colored blocks on the "Greenie Board," which hangs in the squadrons' ready rooms for all to see.

An OK pass is the best—a good approach leading to a three-wire trap. A "fair" pass is safe but with approach deviations, a "no grade" is concerning and, while not actually unsafe, is not good, with big deviations. The worst pass of all is one that is waved off because it was potentially dangerous. An unfortunate pilot with a few of these displayed on the Greenie Board will be attracting a lot of unwanted visibility.

The outboard sections of the Hornet's wings fold vertically upward as, under the guidance of the ever alert yellowshirts, the pilot swiftly taxis the strike-fighter clear of the deck.

Meanwhile, back on the landing-signal platform, every few seconds a voice monotones the phrase "fouled deck." In response to this information the LSO and his deputies hold their pickle switches aloft, aching arms a reminder that the deck is currently unfit to receive another aircraft.

Regardless of this fact, the next jet is already well established on its glide slope. In the cockpit of the approaching A-6 Intruder, the pilot calls the ball. "Roger ball," replies the LSO, his exacting eyes focused on the bomber, ready to wave off the descending A-6 if the deck remains fouled. Paddles turns to glance back along the deck, just in time to see the F/A-18 clear the foul line. An immediate cry of "clear deck" confirms the OK status, permitting the LSO to lower his arm together with the pickle switch.

With trailing-edge flaps and leading-edge slats extended, an A-6 Intruder is well established on its glide slope and only seconds from slamming down onto the GW's deck. Unlike land-based aircraft, which flare, holding off and gently making contact with the runway, carrier-based aircraft maintain a constant angle of attack and glide slope all the way down, intercepting the deck en route. This particularly violent means of recovery permits a much higher degree of accuracy in selecting the exact touch-down point.

Watched intently by the LSOs from their exposed platform, an F/A-18 crosses the carrier's fantail and prepares to contact the deck. The way a pilot "flies the ship" can make or break his career, the most tricky bit being landing back aboard—particularly at night. All approaches and traps are graded by the LSO, a veteran carrier pilot himself, the results displayed for all to see in the various squadron ready rooms. There's a lot of visibility involved and career-minded naval aviators fight not to be the "anchor" man on that list.

Within the approaching Intruder's cockpit, the pilot's workload has been high, the old-generation, low-technology aircraft requiring more input and skill to land than newer user friendly jets such as the Hornet. Initially, the pilot had noted the amber meat-ball beneath the LLD's green datum, indicating he was a little low. But an early correction, a small increase in power and adjustment of attitude has tidied the glide slope and he's now in the groove and looking good, riding the centered ball down.

Seconds later the bomber slams onto the deck, the impact sending a shudder throughout the carrier. The aircraft's beefed-up undercarriage accepts this violent means of arrival with disdain, as it has done similarly many times before. Unlike his land-locked brethren, the carrier pilot does not flare his aircraft on landing but rather flies it "through" the deck, maintaining constant glide slope and angle of attack until the deck intercepts the jet's path. This method permits a much higher degree of accuracy in controlling and predicting the aircraft's exact touch-down point.

The instant the Intruder makes contact with the deck, the pilot moves his throttles to full power in anticipation of a "bolter" or go-around, the result of missing all four wires. A wave-off or bolter does not please the air boss. The pilot will need to make another circuit, the accumulated time adding to the duration of the recovery cycle and the carrier's predictability.

But this Intruder pilot has got it nailed pretty well, and he and his bombardier/navigator are thrown forward against the restraint of their harnesses by the violent deceleration as the jet's hook engages the four wire. A four instead of three, indicating that perhaps he was just a couple of feet high.

It was in the 1920s that exploratory use of cables to arrest a landing aircraft's progress were first tested. Then, the speeds and weights of aircraft were rather inferior to those of today, and the first arresting gear simply consisted of ropes with sandbags attached to each end. Since those early trials, the system has progressed and developed somewhat into the rapid and highly efficient means of trapping aircraft we see today.

The modern arrestor-gear system consists of two "purchase" cables, normally invisible below the deck, which are connected by the actual arrestor cable itself. This is the "cross-deck pendant," a cable 1⅜ inch thick, with a "life" of just 100 arrested landings. The two purchase cables feed below the deck, parallel with the runway, into two long cylinders within the arrestor-gear engine.

In action, when an aircraft's hook snags the cross-deck pendant, the two purchase cables are forced out by the inertia of the aircraft. This in turn pulls shims within the left and right cylinders, which forces fluid through a variable-diameter orifice. The size of the orifice, and therefore resistance incurred, is preset for the type and weight of the landing aircraft. The larger and heavier the aircraft, the smaller the orifice, and therefore the more resistance encountered and vice-versa. The net result is that each aircraft should achieve a similar ideal landing run of around 320 feet. As with catapult launches, the correct weight setting is imperative. Too much resistance and the jet's progress will be arrested too rapidly, risking structural damage. Too little and it could end up perilously close to the bow.

Carrier landings may be difficult but many experienced naval aviators actually enjoy flying the ship, and a high percentage of daytime approaches end in a successful trap. However, turn out the lights and add a low cloud base, rain, and a moving, heaving deck for good measure, and the situation is one that is altogether different.

Few pilots, even those most experienced, admit to actually enjoying the night carrier landing. Many who fly night missions will be concentrating as much on the fact that they've got to do a night landing as on the mission itself. It's always there nagging at the back of the mind, "I've got to come back. . . ."

Moonlit nights with a clear, defined horizon aren't so bad, but then there are those other nights. You're at altitude flying above a solid overcast and it's just beautiful, with bright moonlight reflecting off the effervescent cloud base. But eventually the dreaded moment arrives, and you descend down through the clouds on instruments. Finally at 1,000 feet the jet breaks clear of the overcast, beneath which it's pitch black and raining. No horizon, no depth perception but, if you're lucky, a dim pinprick of light indicating the presence of the carrier.

From the opposite side of the deck a hook-runner watches an approaching F-14. If the pilot flies the ball correctly, keeping the amber meatball centered between the horizontal line of green datum lights, his tail hook should hit the deck smack in the middle of the cluster of four arresting wires, so that it then catches the third, for an "OK Three" pass in the LSO's notebook. The coiled cable in the foreground, between the third and fourth arresting wires, is for the emergency barricade. This is a 20-foot-high set of nylon webbing that can be rigged across the deck in around two minutes and is designed to trap a jet that for some reason or other cannot accept the conventional arresting wires.

You fly your instruments toward the ship and eventually the lights start to form a shape, familiar only because you've seen them many times before. Experience, however, doesn't belay the mounting concern, the fear. The lights resemble a slightly tapering box with a stalk hanging from the bottom. This is the drop line that descends vertically down the stern of the ship on centerline. To the left of the box is a hint of green and yellow—the meatball.

It's important to use your instruments as well as external visual clues. With no other means of depth perception, it's all too easy to get confused, the mind sometimes playing dangerous tricks. Some pilots see a white vertical box traveling toward them, rather than they toward it. Mesmerized, their concentration lapses, and with no altitude reference other than their instruments within the cockpit, they inexplicably fly into the water, never to be heard of again. It does happen.

Night landings involve a longer approach of around one mile, at which distance the meatball or LLD is indistinct. Consequently, here's where the LSO really earns his paycheck, giving advice on line-up as well as just plain providing confidence. Gradually, at about half a mile distance, the colored lights become discernible, the meatball readable. On the final stages of the approach the "box" of lights starts to accelerate toward you, before finally exploding in a crescendo as the aircraft reaches the deck.

The percentage of first-time traps is considerably reduced during bad-weather night ops and most pilots have had their "night in the barrel." And, if they haven't yet, "there are those that have and those that will!"

One bolter or go-around isn't too concerning, but two or more and people start to pay attention. After two or three the pilot will be getting tense and tired. He'll also be getting low on fuel and will need to be "tanked," or in-flight refueled, from a KA-6, a modified version of the Intruder. This is an exercise that is itself difficult and stressful, particularly at night.

Returning to the carrier, he'll be aware that all eyes will be upon him—the LSO's, air boss's, CAG's, squadron mates'—and this psychological pressure only contributes to the problems he already has. Requiring every ounce of concentration and strength, each approach will gradually drain him, and the more fatigued the pilot gets the harder and more desperate the situation will become.

Eventually, during blue-water ops, when there's no land base within flying distance, as an absolute last resort the aircraft would have to be ditched, an extreme measure that thankfully isn't required too often.

Most times pilots will trap off the first or second approach. However, just when they thought it was all over comes the next scary bit, taxiing around the deck at night. On a really dark one you can't see anything, except that is, for the 19-year-old kid with glow sticks who's guiding the aircraft nearer and nearer to the deck edge. The situation's no problem around the island. There, dull sodium lighting provides a degree of illumination, but way up on the bow, where they always take the Tomcats, it's dark, very dark.

The nose wheel on the F-14 is positioned well aft of the cockpit, and these young guys will wave you so that the tires are within inches of the flight-deck edge, at which time the cockpit is actually swinging out over the water. Ahead and beneath is a black void. One mistake or error in judgment by the young yellow-shirt and it would swallow you up. Almost as scary as a night trap.

But finally you stop, the plane captain signaling to shut down. It's usually around this time, while they're chaining the jet to its spot, that you start to feel the adrenaline, your mouth dry and your legs trembling. Up till now you've been so wrapped up in bringing the jet home that you didn't realize just how much

The Hawkeye is usually one of the last aircraft to recover, but it looks like this pilot has nailed it, the Hummer's tail hook still snagged onto the three wire—an OK pass.

The four arresting wires are separated from each other by a distance of 40 feet. Although this may sound like a lot, when set up on the correct glide slope angle, a height deviation of just a few feet can mean the differences between coming in either too low and taking a one wire or too high and missing all four for a bolter, or overshoot. In anticipation of an overshoot, the instant the jet hits the deck the pilot selects full power. If the aircraft successfully catches a wire, he'll immediately go to idle, and if not, it's back off the deck and in the air before he knows it.

concentration, how much effort was involved. Finally, when you stop, when you relax, it hits you all at once.

Most pilots can't sleep for two or three hours after a night trap because they're just so wound up. Instead, following the obligatory debrief, many are to be found in the early hours munching a "slider" (hamburger) or two before finally escaping to their staterooms for some shuteye.

Meanwhile, back on deck, the tired shirts are completing their respotting exercises in readiness for tomorrow, when the whole cycle of carrier life aboard the USS *George Washington* will unfold once again.

Index